Little
Big Giant

Stories of Wisdom and Inspiration

Michael Jackson

King of Pop

Introduction

As the sun set on June 25, 2009, the world was left in shock as news of Michael Jackson's sudden death spread like wildfire. The King of Pop, known for his iconic music and electrifying performances, had passed away at the age of 50. Fans around the globe mourned the loss of a legend, but what truly captivated the public's attention was the mysterious circumstances surrounding his death.

Jackson's personal physician, Dr. Conrad Murray, had been administering a powerful anesthetic called propofol to help the singer sleep. However, on that fateful day, something went terribly wrong. Murray found Jackson unresponsive and immediately called for help. Despite the efforts of paramedics and hospital staff, Jackson was pronounced dead at 2:26 pm.

The world was left with many questions. How could someone as talented and beloved as Michael Jackson die so suddenly? What role did Dr. Murray play in his death? And most importantly, what really happened behind closed doors in the final moments of the King of Pop's life?

As the investigation into Jackson's death unfolded, more shocking details emerged. It was revealed that the singer had been struggling with a crippling addiction to prescription drugs, and that his health had been deteriorating rapidly. Rumors of foul play and conspiracy theories began to swirl, leaving the public hungry for answers.

But amidst all the speculation and controversy, one thing remained certain: the world had lost a true musical genius. Michael Jackson's legacy would live on through his timeless music, but the mystery surrounding his death would continue to haunt us. What really happened to the King of Pop on that fateful day? Only time would tell.

Table of Contents

Chapter 1

Childhood and Early Beginnings: From

Gary, Indiana to the Jackson 5

Michael Jackson was born on August 29, 1958 in Gary, Indiana. He was the seventh of nine children in the Jackson family. His parents, Joseph and Katherine Jackson, were both musicians and encouraged their children to pursue music as well.

From a young age, Michael showed a natural talent for singing and dancing. He would often imitate famous artists like James Brown and Jackie Wilson, impressing his family and friends with his skills. His father saw potential in Michael and began to train him and his brothers in singing and dancing.

In 1964, Michael's father formed a music group with his five eldest sons, Jackie, Tito, Jermaine, Marlon, and Michael. They called themselves the Jackson 5 and began performing at local talent shows and clubs. Michael, at just six years old, was the lead singer of the group and quickly became the star of the show with his powerful voice and energetic dance moves.

The Jackson 5 caught the attention of record label Motown Records and were signed in 1968. Their first four singles, "I Want You Back," "ABC," "The Love You Save," and "I'll Be There," all reached number one on the Billboard Hot 100 chart, making them the first group to achieve this feat. The Jackson 5 became an instant sensation and Michael, at only 11 years old, was already a household name.

Despite their success, the Jackson 5 continued to work hard and tour extensively. They performed all over the world, including in Europe and Asia, and were loved by fans of all ages. Michael's performances were electrifying, with his signature dance moves and soulful voice captivating audiences everywhere.

Key Takeaway: Michael Jackson's childhood and early beginnings were filled with hard work, dedication, and a natural talent for music. He showed that with determination and support from his family, he was able to achieve great success at a young age.

Chapter 2

Rising Stardom: The Jackson 5's Success

and Michael's Solo Career

As Michael Jackson grew older, his talent and passion for music only continued to grow. He was no longer just a cute little boy with a big voice, but a rising star in the music industry. Along with his brothers, Michael became a part of the famous group, The Jackson 5.

The Jackson 5 consisted of five brothers: Jackie, Tito, Jermaine, Marlon, and of course, Michael. They were all incredibly talented and together, they created a unique sound that captivated audiences all over the world. With their catchy songs and synchronized dance moves, they quickly became a sensation.

Their first single, "I Want You Back," was released in 1969 and became an instant hit. It reached number one on the charts and launched the Jackson 5 into stardom. They followed up with more hit songs like "ABC" and "The Love You Save," solidifying their place in the music industry.

But it was Michael's solo career that truly set him apart from his brothers. In 1971, at just 13 years old, he released his first solo album, "Got to Be There." The album featured his hit single, "Ben," which reached number one on the charts. Michael's voice and performance skills were praised by critics and fans alike.

As Michael's solo career took off, he continued to release hit after hit. In 1982, he released his most successful album to date, "Thriller." It became the best-selling album of all time, with over 66 million copies sold worldwide. Songs like "Billie Jean" and "Beat It" topped the charts and Michael's iconic music videos revolutionized the music industry.

Despite his success, Michael remained humble and dedicated to his craft. He continued to push boundaries and create music that touched the hearts of millions. His performances were electrifying and his dance moves were unmatched. He became known as the "King of Pop" and his influence on the music industry is still felt today.

Key Takeaway:

Michael Jackson's success as a solo artist was a result of his hard work, dedication, and passion for music. He never let his fame get to his head and always stayed true to himself. His talent and determination are an inspiration to us all.

Chapter 3

Thriller: The Best-Selling Album of All Time

It was the year 1982, and the world was about to witness the release of an album that would change the music industry forever. The artist behind this masterpiece was none other than the King of Pop himself, Michael Jackson. With his previous albums already achieving great success, the expectations were high for his upcoming release.

But little did anyone know, this album would go on to become the best-selling album of all time, with over 66 million copies sold worldwide. It was none other than "Thriller."

The album was a perfect blend of pop, rock, and funk, with each song showcasing Michael's incredible vocal range and dance moves. The lead single, "Thriller," was a 14-minute music video that revolutionized the music industry. With its spooky theme and iconic choreography, it became an instant hit and is still considered one of the greatest music videos of all time.

But it wasn't just the title track that made this album a huge success. Each song on the album was a hit in its own right. From the catchy beats of "Beat It" to the emotional ballad "Human Nature," each song had its own unique charm that captivated listeners worldwide.

"Thriller" not only topped the charts but also broke barriers. It was the first album by a black artist to receive heavy rotation on MTV, which was a predominantly white music channel at the time. This opened doors for more diversity in the music industry and paved the way for other artists of color to achieve success.

The album also won a record-breaking eight Grammy Awards, including Album of the Year. It was a testament to Michael's incredible talent and hard work that went into creating this masterpiece.

Even after 39 years, "Thriller" continues to be a best-selling album, with new generations discovering and falling in love with it. Its impact on the music industry and popular culture is undeniable, making it a timeless classic.

Key Takeaway:

"Thriller" is not just an album, it's a cultural phenomenon. It showed the world that music has no boundaries and that true talent knows no color. It also taught us that hard work and dedication can lead to great success. And most importantly, it reminded us that good music never goes out of style.

Chapter 4

Controversies and Criticism: Michael's Changing Appearance and Personal Life

As Michael Jackson's fame and success continued to grow, so did the public's fascination with his personal life. And with that fascination came intense scrutiny and criticism, especially when it came to his changing appearance.

In the early 1980s, Michael's appearance began to change drastically. His skin became lighter, his nose appeared smaller, and his facial features seemed to be constantly evolving. This sparked rumors and speculation about the reasons behind his transformation.

Some people believed that Michael was trying to erase his African American heritage and conform to Western beauty standards. Others speculated that he was suffering from a skin condition called vitiligo, which causes patches of skin to lose their pigment. Despite Michael's explanation that he had the condition, many still doubted and criticized him.

In addition to his physical appearance, Michael's personal life also faced intense scrutiny. He was often portrayed as eccentric and reclusive, with rumors of his bizarre behavior and extravagant spending habits. His relationships with children, including his own children and his close friendships with young boys, also drew criticism and raised questions.

One of the most controversial moments in Michael's personal life came in 1993 when he was accused of child sexual abuse by a 13-year-old boy. The media frenzy surrounding the case was intense and Michael's reputation was tarnished. However, he maintained his innocence and the case was eventually settled out of court.

Despite the controversies and criticism, Michael continued to focus on his music and his humanitarian efforts. He used his platform and wealth to support various charities and raise awareness for important causes. However, the negative attention and constant scrutiny took a toll on his mental and physical health.

Key Takeaway: It's important to remember that celebrities are human beings too and they have their own struggles and challenges. It's important to treat others with kindness and empathy, rather than judging them based on rumors and speculation.

Chapter 5

Moonwalk: The Iconic Dance Move and

World Tour

Michael Jackson's career was skyrocketing to new heights as he released his hit album "Thriller" in 1982. Along with the album's success, Jackson also introduced the world to a new dance move that would become his signature and forever be associated with his name - the Moonwalk.

The Moonwalk was first performed by Jackson during a performance of "Billie Jean" on the TV special "Motown 25:

Yesterday, Today, Forever" in 1983. It was a move that seemed to defy gravity, as Jackson appeared to glide backwards while still moving forward. The audience was stunned and the Moonwalk quickly became a sensation.

The dance move was actually not a new invention by Jackson. It had been around since the 1930s and was known as the "backslide" or the "back step". However, Jackson's smooth execution and popularization of the move made it iconic and synonymous with his name.

The Moonwalk was not the only dance move that Jackson popularized during this time. He also introduced the "robot" and the "moonwalk spin" which were both incorporated into his performances and music videos. Jackson's unique and mesmerizing dance moves captured the attention of the world and solidified his status as the King of Pop.

In addition to the Moonwalk, Jackson's "Thriller" album also spawned a world tour that would become one of the most successful and iconic tours in music history. The tour, aptly named "The Victory Tour", featured Jackson and his brothers performing to sold-out stadiums and arenas across the globe.

The tour was not without its challenges, as Jackson struggled with the pressure of being the lead performer and the constant media attention. However, he persevered and delivered electrifying performances that left audiences in awe.

One of the most memorable moments of the tour was when Jackson performed the Moonwalk during his hit song "Billie Jean". The crowd went wild as they witnessed the iconic dance move in person. The tour was a huge success, grossing over $75 million and solidifying Jackson's status as a global superstar.

Key Takeaway: The Moonwalk and the "Victory Tour" were two defining moments in Michael Jackson's career. They showcased his unparalleled talent and cemented his place in music history. These events also taught us that with hard work, perseverance, and dedication, we can achieve our dreams and leave a lasting impact on the world.

Chapter 6

Humanitarian Work: Michael's Contributions to Charity and Philanthropy

Michael Jackson was not only a talented musician and performer, but he was also a kind and generous person who dedicated much of his life to helping others. Throughout his career, he used his fame and fortune to make a positive impact on the world through his numerous charitable contributions and philanthropic efforts.

One of Michael's most well-known contributions to charity was his involvement with the organization, "We Are the World." In 1985, he co-wrote and recorded the hit song with other famous artists to raise money for famine relief in Africa. The song was a huge success and raised over $63 million for charity.

In addition to his involvement with "We Are the World," Michael also donated millions of dollars to various charities and organizations, including the Make-A-Wish Foundation, the Elizabeth Taylor AIDS Foundation, and the Children's Defense

Fund. He also supported numerous children's hospitals and orphanages around the world, often visiting them and spending time with the children.

But Michael's philanthropy went beyond just donating money. He was also a strong advocate for children's rights and worked tirelessly to improve the lives of children in need. In 1992, he founded the Heal the World Foundation, which focused on providing healthcare, education, and other resources to underprivileged children around the world.

One of Michael's most memorable acts of philanthropy was his visit to Romania in 1992. He was deeply moved by the poverty and suffering he witnessed there, and he immediately took action. He donated millions of dollars to build a children's hospital and orphanage in Bucharest, and he also personally visited and spent time with the children there.

Michael's humanitarian work extended beyond just children's causes. He was also a strong advocate for the environment and animal welfare. He often spoke out against pollution and deforestation and was a supporter of various wildlife conservation organizations.

Key Takeaway: Michael Jackson's contributions to charity and philanthropy serve as a reminder that even the smallest acts of kindness can make a big difference in the world. He showed us that we all have the power to make a positive impact and help those in need, no matter our age or background.

Chapter 7

Neverland Ranch: The Private World of

Michael Jackson

Michael Jackson was not just a talented singer and dancer, he was also a visionary. He had a dream of creating a magical place where he could escape from the pressures of fame and be a kid again. And so, in 1988, he purchased a 2,700-acre property in Santa Barbara County, California, and named it Neverland Ranch.

The ranch was not just a regular home, it was a private world that Michael had designed to reflect his love for fairytales and amusement parks. There was a grand entrance with a clock tower, a train station, and a floral clock. The main house, called the "castle," had six bedrooms and nine bathrooms. It was filled with elaborate furnishings, including a throne room and a secret room hidden behind a bookshelf.

But the real magic of Neverland Ranch was in its outdoor attractions. There was a petting zoo with exotic animals like elephants, giraffes, and tigers. Michael also had his own personal zoo with llamas, alpacas, and even a giraffe named Jabbar. There were also rides and games, like a carousel, a Ferris wheel, and a bumper car track. And let's not forget the iconic Neverland Ranch train, which took visitors on a tour around the property.

But Neverland Ranch was not just for fun and games. Michael also used it to give back to the community. He often invited sick and underprivileged children to visit and enjoy the ranch. He also hosted charity events and donated millions of dollars to various organizations.

Unfortunately, Neverland Ranch also became a place of controversy. In 1993, Michael was accused of child sexual abuse by a young boy who had visited the ranch. The accusations were later settled out of court, but the ranch was searched by police and became a media frenzy. In 2003, Michael faced similar charges from another young boy and the ranch was again searched. This time, Michael was arrested and later acquitted of all charges.

After the trials, Michael felt like
Neverland Ranch was no longer a place of
happiness for him. He closed the ranch to
the public and eventually moved out. In
2008, the ranch was facing foreclosure and
Michael had to sell it to a real estate
investment firm.

Key Takeaway: Neverland Ranch was a
place where Michael Jackson could escape
from the pressures of fame and be a kid
again. It was a magical world filled with
amusement park attractions and exotic
animals. But it also became a place of

controversy and ultimately led to the downfall of Michael's beloved home.

Chapter 8

Super Bowl Halftime Show: The

Most-Watched Performance in History

It was February 1, 2004, and all eyes were on the Super Bowl. But it wasn't just the game that had everyone talking. It was the halftime show, and this year, it was going to be a performance that would go down in history.

The crowd was buzzing with excitement as they waited for the show to begin. Suddenly, the stadium went dark and the sound of drums filled the air. The audience was on their feet as the King of

Pop, Michael Jackson, appeared on stage in a sparkling silver suit. The energy in the stadium was electric as he began to sing his hit song, "Billie Jean."

The stage was transformed into a magical wonderland as Jackson danced and sang, mesmerizing the audience with his iconic moves. He was joined by a group of dancers who moved in perfect synchronization with him. It was like watching a real-life music video.

As the performance continued, Jackson sang some of his other popular songs like "Black or White" and "Heal the World." The audience sang along, their voices echoing throughout the stadium. It was a moment of unity and joy, as people from all walks of life came together to celebrate the music of Michael Jackson.

But the highlight of the show came when Jackson performed his signature move, the moonwalk. The crowd erupted in cheers and applause as he glided across the stage, showing off his incredible talent and showmanship.

The performance ended with a spectacular fireworks display and the entire stadium chanting "Michael! Michael!" It was a moment that would be remembered forever, not just as a Super Bowl halftime show, but as one of the greatest performances in history.

Key Takeaway: Michael Jackson's Super Bowl halftime show was more than just a performance, it was a moment of unity and celebration of music. It showed the world the power of music to bring people together and create unforgettable

memories.

.

Chapter 9

Legal Battles: Accusations and Trials

As Michael Jackson's fame and success continued to rise, so did the number of legal battles he faced. In the 1990s, he was accused of child sexual abuse, which sparked a series of highly publicized trials and legal battles that would haunt him for the rest of his life.

The first accusation came in 1993, when a 13-year-old boy named Jordan Chandler accused Jackson of molesting him. This led to a civil lawsuit against

Jackson, which was eventually settled out of court for a reported $22 million. However, the damage to Jackson's reputation had already been done.

In 2003, another accusation of child sexual abuse was made against Jackson, this time by a 12-year-old boy named Gavin Arvizo. This accusation led to a highly publicized trial, where Jackson was eventually acquitted of all charges in 2005. Despite the not guilty verdict, the media frenzy and negative publicity surrounding the trial took a toll on Jackson's mental and physical health.

But the legal battles didn't end there. In 2006, Jackson faced another lawsuit from a former employee, accusing him of unpaid wages and emotional distress. The case was settled out of court for an undisclosed amount.

In 2009, just months before his death, Jackson faced yet another legal battle. This time, he was sued by concert promoter AEG Live for breach of contract, claiming that Jackson had failed to fulfill his obligations for a series of comeback concerts. The trial was set to begin in 2011, but was ultimately settled out of court for an undisclosed amount.

Despite the numerous legal battles he faced, Jackson always maintained his innocence and denied all accusations against him. However, the constant scrutiny and negative publicity took a toll on his mental and physical health, leading to a spiral of addiction and eventually his untimely death in 2009.

Key Takeaway: Legal battles can have a major impact on one's life, regardless of the outcome. It's important to always stand up for yourself and your beliefs, but also to be aware of the potential consequences of being in the public eye.

Chapter 10

Legacy: Remembering the King of Pop
and His Impact on Music and Culture

As the news of Michael Jackson's passing spread around the world, fans and music lovers everywhere mourned the loss of the King of Pop. But even in death, Michael's legacy lives on, leaving an indelible mark on the music industry and popular culture.

Michael Jackson's music was unlike anything the world had ever heard before.

His smooth vocals, electrifying dance moves, and innovative music videos captivated audiences and broke barriers. Songs like "Thriller," "Beat It," and "Billie Jean" became instant classics and solidified Michael's place in music history.

But Michael's impact went beyond just his music. He was a trailblazer in many ways, breaking racial barriers and using his platform to spread messages of love, unity, and social change. He was also a philanthropist, using his fame and fortune to support various charities and humanitarian causes.

One of Michael's most significant contributions to music was his influence on future generations of artists. Many of today's biggest stars, such as Beyoncé, Justin Timberlake, and Bruno Mars, credit Michael as their inspiration and cite his music as a major influence on their own.

Michael's impact on popular culture cannot be overstated. He revolutionized the music video industry, elevating it to an art form with his elaborate and cinematic productions. His fashion choices, from his iconic red leather jacket to his signature white glove, became fashion trends that people still emulate today.

Key Takeaway: Michael Jackson's legacy is one of creativity, innovation, and breaking barriers. His impact on music and popular culture continues to be felt even after his passing, and his influence on future generations of artists is undeniable. He will always be remembered as the King of Pop and a true music icon.

Dear Reader,

Thank you for choosing "Little Big Giant - Stories of Wisdom and Inspiration"! We hope this book has inspired and motivated you on your own journey to success.

If you enjoyed reading this book and believe in the power of its message, we kindly ask for your support. Please consider leaving a positive review on the platform where you purchased the book. Your review will help spread the message to more young readers, empowering them to dream big and achieve greatness. We acknowledge that mistakes can happen, and we appreciate your forgiveness.

Remember, the overall message of this book is the key. Thank you for being a part of our mission to inspire and uplift young minds.

Made in the USA
Las Vegas, NV
15 April 2025

21002314R00046